RAINFOREST

Earth's Ecosystems

Francie Dolan

Norwood House Press

Cataloging-in-Publication Data

Names: Dolan, Francie.
Title: Rainforest / Francie Dolan.
Description: Buffalo, NY : Norwood House Press, 2026. | Series: Earth's ecosystems | Includes glossary and index.
Identifiers: ISBN 9781978577046 (pbk.) | ISBN 9781978577053 (library bound) | ISBN 9781978577060 (ebook)
Subjects: LCSH: Rain forest ecology--Juvenile literature. | Rain forests--Juvenile literature.
Classification: LCC QH541.5.R27 D65 2026 | DDC 577.34--dc23

Published in 2026 by
Norwood House Press
2544 Clinton Street
Buffalo, NY 14224

Designer: Rhea Magaro
Editor: Kim Thompson

Photo credits: Cover, p. 1 MILAGO, Kumer Oksana/Shutterstock.com; p. 3 Reforestation Collection/Shutterstock.com; p. 5 Philipp Edler/Shutterstock.com; p. 6 MatteoFar8/Shutterstock.com; p. 7 Teo Tarras/Shutterstock.com; p. 9 Danita Delimont/Shutterstock.com; p. 10 Taylor Beaty/Shutterstock.com; p. 12 Manzooranmai/Shutterstock.com; p. 13 acceptphoto/Shutterstock.com; p. 14 Alexwilko/Shutterstock.com; p. 15 Hari Gopalakrishnen/Shutterstock.com; p. 16 Raseduly/Shutterstock.com; p. 17 Foto 4440/Shutterstock.com; p. 19 Mark_Kostich/Shutterstock.com; p. 19 BAUER Alexandre/Shutterstock.com; p. 20 Baurz1973/Shutterstock.com; p. 21 BorneoRimbawan/Shutterstock.com

Printed in the United States of America

CPSIA compliance information: Batch #CWNHP26: For further information contact Norwood House Press at 1-800-237-9932.

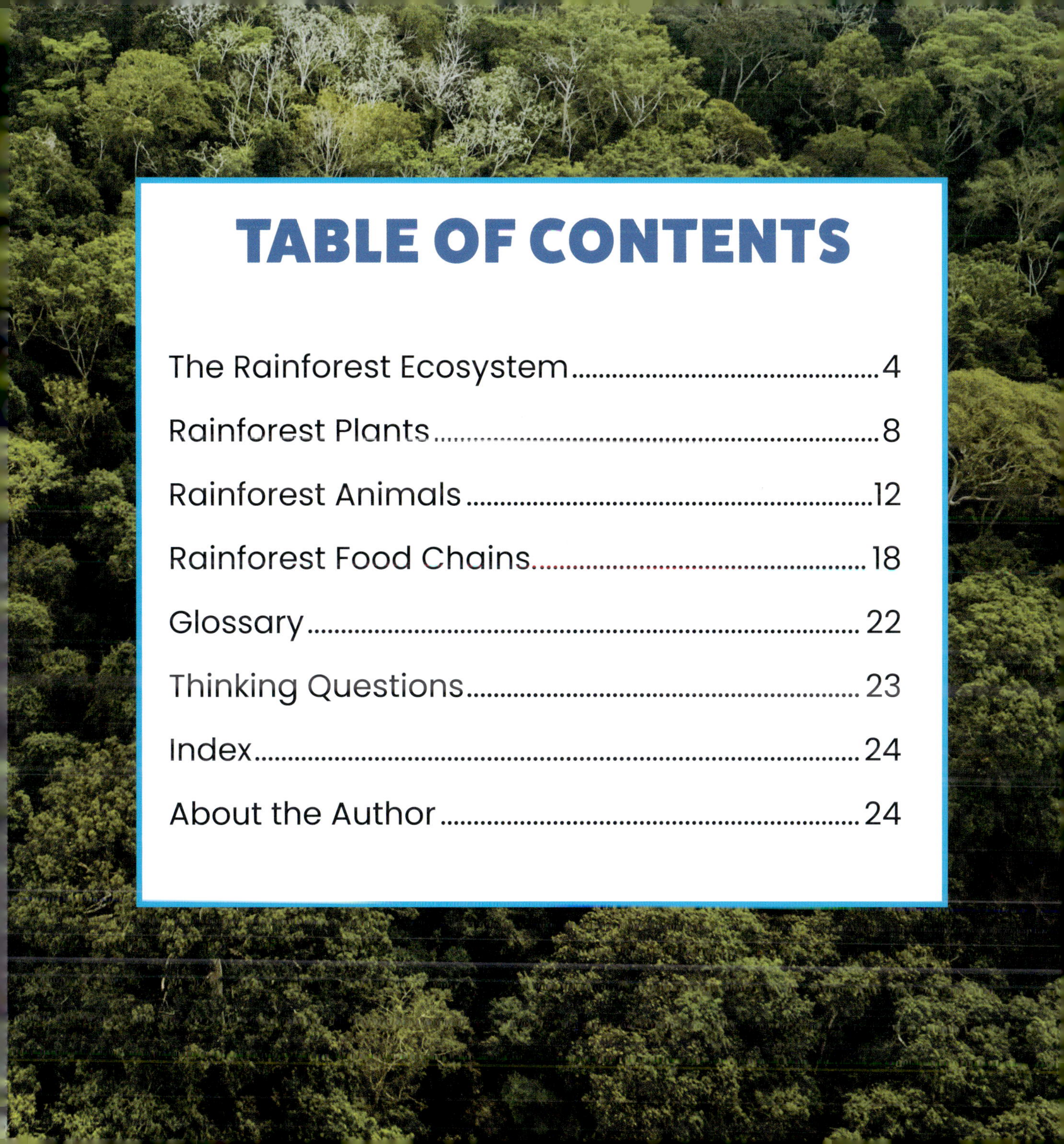

TABLE OF CONTENTS

The Rainforest Ecosystem

Eco- means "home" or "environment." *System* means "a group of things that work together." Earth has many **ecosystems** that support life. Each is home to a network of living things that depend on each other.

One kind of ecosystem is a rainforest. Rainforests are the wettest forests on the planet. Most are in the **tropics**. The warm, wet rainforests near the **equator** get more than six feet (two meters) of rain each year.

Rainforests are found all over the world. The largest is the Amazon Rainforest in South America. It is as big as the United States without Alaska and Hawaii.

Rainforests cover just six percent of Earth's surface, but they have incredible **biodiversity**. Half of all plant and animal **species** live in rainforests.

Rainforest Plants

Rainforests are dense and green. They are home to hundreds of thousands of plant species.

Rainforest trees **compete** for sunlight. Giant kapok trees can stretch 200 feet (60 meters) tall. Their flowers and fruits feed bats and other animals.

Colorful orchids and bromeliads bloom in the rainforest. Thick, woody vines called lianas grow among the trees. They form a network across the forest. Spider monkeys and other animals travel on this vine "highway."

Rainforest Animals

Animals live in all four layers of the rainforest.

The **emergent layer** is in the treetops. It is home to many birds. Harpy eagles make their nests here. Scarlet macaws gather in noisy groups.

Most rainforest animals live in the next layer down, the **canopy**. It is home to animals that climb, glide, and fly. There is plenty of food, including fruits, nuts, and leaves.

In Southeastern Asian rainforests, orangutans swing through the canopy. They rarely touch the ground.

Below the canopy is the dimly-lit **understory**. Blue morpho butterflies flit by. Boa constrictors hide. Poison dart frogs jump on mossy rocks.

The bottom layer of the rainforest is the forest floor. In this dark region, dead leaves pile up. Ants and other insects scurry by. Jaguars are on the prowl.

Rainforest Food Chains

In a rainforest, living things eat other living things in food chains. An **agouti** might feed on Brazil nuts. An anaconda may eat the agouti. After the anaconda dies, its remains may be eaten by beetles on the forest floor.

Many rainforest food chains together form a food web. It shows how all living things in a rainforest ecosystem depend on each other for survival.

RAINFOREST FOOD WEB

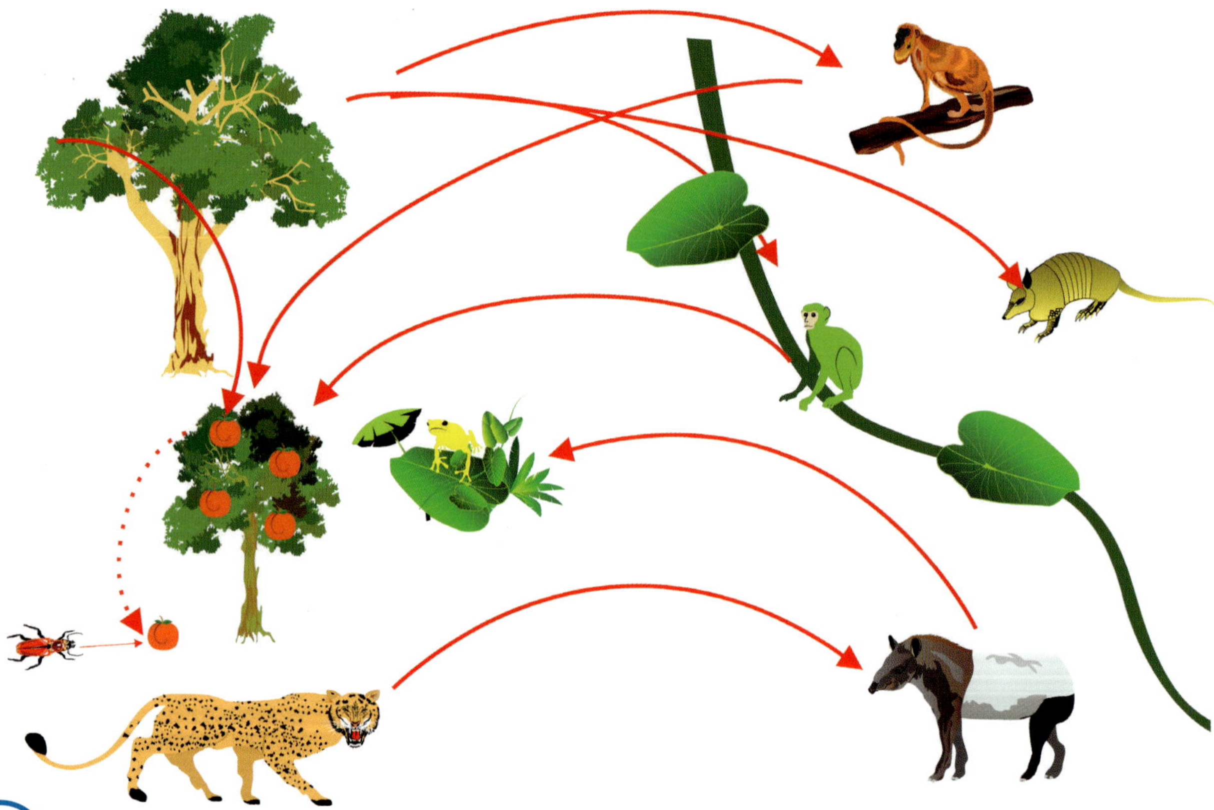

Glossary

agouti (uh-GOO-tee): a tropical rodent that is about the same size as a rabbit

biodiversity (bye-oh-duh-VUR-si-tee): a wide variety of species living in a single area

canopy (KAN-uh-pee): the second-highest level of a rainforest that is made up of branches, vines, and leaves and where most rainforest animals live

compete (kuhm-PEET): to try hard to get resources or to win over others

ecosystems (EE-koh-sis-tuhms): natural communities where plants, animals, and their environment all work together

emergent layer (i-MUR-juhnt LAY-ur): the uppermost layer of a rainforest where the tops of the tallest trees emerge from the dense plants below

equator (i-KWAY-tur): the imaginary line around the center of Earth that is an equal distance away from the North Pole and South Pole

species (SPEE-sheez): a group of living things that are alike and can reproduce together

tropics (TRAH-piks): the hot areas near Earth's equator that get lots of sunlight

understory (UHN-dur-stor-ee): the rainforest layer between the forest floor and the canopy where there is little sunlight and where shrubs, ferns, moss, and young trees grow

Thinking Questions

1. What is an ecosystem?
2. Describe a rainforest.
3. What kinds of animals live in the rainforest canopy?
4. Why do you think the rainforest understory is dark?
5. What does a food chain show?

Index

About the Author

Francie Dolan is continually amazed by the natural world and how Earth's plants, animals, and natural resources are interconnected. From her home near Seattle, Washington, she loves to hike and explore forests, lakes, mountains, and the seashore. When she gets home, she likes to draw and write about what she sees on her adventures.